UNDERSTANDING DRUGS

INHALANTS

Mark Pownall

GLOUCESTER PRESS
London · New York · Toronto · Sydney

INTRODUCTION

Inhalants are the available drugs. Every home contains substances such as glues, aerosols and paints which give off vapours that can be sniffed. Every car petrol tank is a potential source of vapour, and every office uses typewriter correction fluids which are useful when wiping out a mistake, but which can be deadly when wiping out reality in a sniffing session.

An "inhalant" is any substance that gives off a gas (vapour or fumes) which can be breathed deep into the lungs. Someone who sniffs glue does not breathe in the glue itself but the solvent, the substance in which the glue is dissolved. Many inhaled chemicals are solvents. They pass through the thin lung lining into the blood, and then get carried to the brain, where they have their effects.

The number of everyday products that can be abused by inhaling as a drug is countless. One youth club, concerned that its members were using inhalants, drew up a list of "sniffable" substances. There were more than a hundred. As soon as these were banned, others took their place.

Street supplies of other drugs such as heroin and amphetamines dry up from time to time, or the price may go up because of short supply. But people intent on getting a

Some inhalent abusers may become aggressive when under the influence.

buzz from inhalants will nearly always be able to get hold of something, however careful shopkeepers may be in their sales of glue, aerosols, varnishes, solvents, paints and similar substances. Restricted selling, to people who will use them only for their proper purpose, is virtually impossible.

Mention inhalant or solvent abuse and people tend to think of groups of teenage delinquents sitting around in a derelict house, breathing in fumes from crisp bags full of glue. This is the picture we have from the horror stories in magazines and newspapers and on television.

But is it true? Which kinds of people use glue, solvents and other inhalants, and why do they do it? Is it just a passing fad, or a sign of some deep-rooted problem? And do newspaper and TV stories encourage certain people to begin using inhalants?

This book looks behind the often misleading headlines at who really takes inhalants, why they do it, and the harm these substances can do. For those who get into trouble there is help available. Users often say that they sniff to escape, or forget, or block out the problems of life. But in the long run, any form of drug abuse is simply adding another problem to your life.

❝ *I hated school, and home was boring. Glue seemed the only thing to do, the only excitement.* **❞**

WHY DO PEOPLE ABUS INHALANTS?

" *It makes me feel good. I'm not afraid when I'm under.* **"**

A few of the people caught up in the inhalants scene do fit the popular picture of "glue-sniffers". They dress as punks or in some other conspicuous way, sniff and inhale to get out of their heads, and then become abusive and aggressive and perhaps violent.

Some of these people come from poor and often unhappy backgrounds. Maybe they have an alcoholic parent, or there is arguing and violence at home. But this is not the whole answer. Most people who use inhalants are teenagers, and most of these are normal and healthy, from ordinary backgrounds.

They seem to become involved for many different reasons. Perhaps curiosity, or a chance encounter, or pressure put on them by friends. Some do it simply for the effect of the inhalant drug on the brain, which makes them feel "high" or "stoned", or gives them a "buzz", or puts them "up" or "under". Others do it to escape from everyday life, or because it is risky and daring.

A passing fad

Surveys about inhalant use show that most young people know inhalants are dangerous. Those who try inhaling soon stop. For the vast majority, inhalants are just a passing fad, a way of keeping in with mates or proving toughness to the gang. They soon fade away and are forgotten.

However some people don't fully understand what inhalants can and can't do. One 12-year-old boy, whose

The boredom of city tower-block life may encourage drug experimentation.

mother had died two years ago, was found sniffing dry-cleaning fluid alone in his bedroom. When asked why, he said he'd been told that people saw things when they sniffed dry-cleaning fluid. He desperately wanted to see his mother again.

Staying in with the gang

Pressure from friends has an important influence on teenagers, and even more so on younger children. In one case a nine-year-old boy joined a gang of older boys. They would only let him stay if he agreed to sniff glue with them. He did so, but soon afterwards he made friends of his own age. The new friends accepted him for what he was, not for what he could be forced into doing. He soon lost interest in trying to impress the older gang and he stopped inhaling.

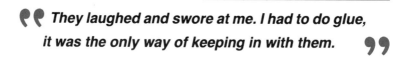

❝❝ *They laughed and swore at me. I had to do glue, it was the only way of keeping in with them.* 💬

This shows how cruel the pressure of a group can be. A gang can use inhalants as a way of keeping out unwanted people or making them "prove" themselves.

Cheap, available and reliable?

For some it's the cheapness of inhalants, compared to other illegal drugs like heroin, which encourages them to experiment. The cost of inhalant abuse becomes clear when you consider that one bottle of varnish remover can get more people "drunk" than a gallon of cheap wine.

Unlike some street drugs, there is always a good supply of substances that can be inhaled, at the corner hardware shop or in the supermarket. This is not quite so true today, as shopkeepers restrict their sales and become wise to the tricks of those wanting to abuse, not use.

Another "advantage" of inhalants is that they can be carried about so easily. They are everyday items which don't make people suspicious. Again, this is not so true nowadays. Many parents, teachers, police officers and others have a fair idea of which substances can be inhaled.

Glue, varnish, aerosols and paint usually come in convenient cans or packets. A bottle of nail polish remover or a tube of adhesive is much easier to hide than a bottle of cider. If it's discovered, there is a chance that it can be explained away more easily.

The high of glue solvent or a similar inhaled chemical can be more reliable than with a street drug like marijuana, whose quality varies so much. However the reliability of inhalants comes only with practice, which is a dangerous part of the way towards heavy and regular use with its various health risks.

Getting "high"

Some people who use drugs say they do it to change the way they feel. They want to think different thoughts and have different experiences from those in everday life. Some people who experiment with inhalants also give this reason.

The chemicals in glue, aerosols and similar inhalants act as drugs to alter the state of the mind, and this appeals to certain users. They want to get high or stoned, they want the buzz. Some say they feel pleasant emotional sensations. Others describe their feelings as floating about without a care in the world. Yet others say the drugs in inhalants blot out everything unpleasant.

❝ It makes me feel good. I'm not afraid when I'm under. ❞

It's a quick way to being drunk

Many inhalant users say that being high on inhalants is like being drunk. But sniffing is different to drinking in that the effects are much faster. Inhalation allows the vapours to go into the blood surrounding the lungs in a few seconds, and from there to the brain is only a few seconds more. There is no waiting for alcohol to be absorbed in the gut as there is with drink.

Sadly it is this quick action, affecting the user's brain before he or she realises it, that causes so many tragic accidents.

Sniffing may be part of a general "rebellion" in clothes and hair style.

The feelings of drunkenness are also over quicker with inhalants, compared to alcohol. The effects last on average about an hour, rather than several hours as with drink.

Life seems so boring . . .

Many inhalant users are not that interested in getting high. The appeal is to do something exciting and dangerous, something of which other people disapprove. Many experts say that boredom is a common reason why young people start sniffing.

Tied up with this is the reason that glue sniffing can be used to shock other people. It can be a way of rebelling

Some people turn to solvents while others use alcohol or tobacco.

against parents, teachers or anyone in authority. In general, inhalants can be used to annoy – especially the older generation, who are familiar with drugs like tobacco and alcohol, but not with glue or solvents. Some adults may over-react if faced with young people using inhalants.

> *Young people who are not doing well at school feel they are wasting their time, and so they prefer to play truant and look for excitement elsewhere.*
>
> **(James Balding, US Solvent Abuse Helpline.)**

Three types of inhalant user?

Young people give a variety of reasons why they sniff. In one survey, more than 4,000 children (some who used inhalants, some who didn't) were asked what they thought. Over a third of the group reckoned that people abused solvents to copy their friends. Other reasons which they thought were important were depression, boredom and wanting to get high. Another reason was publicity given to glue sniffing, in the papers or on TV. Some people copied the sniffing in the hope of attracting the same sort of attention, becoming "famous".

All these influences appear to act together to produce

A common "sniffers' corner" – a run-down but secluded corner.

broadly three types of inhalant user. One is the "experimental" type who inhales with friends to be sociable and stay as part of a group. He (it's usually a boy) never becomes too involved, and stops after a few weeks.

The second type, similar to the first, is perhaps a little more unsure of himself. He likes the approval of his friends, and he enjoys the company and support of a "glue group" in which he can get stoned. He uses inhalants more often, maybe a couple of times a week over several months. Even so, the amount of inhaling, and the time for which the substances are sniffed, is low.

People in the third and smallest group run the greatest risks. At first they are in the first two groups, but then inhaling becomes more important. They begin to use the drugs to hide from real life and its problems. This slide into depending on inhalants can happen to anyone – you can't predict who will be affected and who will stay clear.

There are a few inhalant abusers who get into really heavy use. For them, inhalants become more than a way of getting a few thrills, they are all that life offers. Such people don't appear to be able to face life "sober", perhaps because of upsets at home, trouble at school, the boredom of not having a job, and so on.

This small group includes those who inhale alone, and those who continue to inhale after their friends have given it up as a passing fad. They may join others to form a group which meets regularly just to get high, often stealing the glue or whatever they use. They are on the way to becoming dependent on inhalants.

In general terms, the average inhalant abuser is in his early teens. He may sniff once or twice a week, for several weeks or a few months. He then gives it up. Experts have noted that very few people over the age of about 16 or 17 continue sniffing. It may be more than coincidence that this is the age at which many people begin to go into pubs and clubs and drink alcohol. It has been suggested that some inhalant abusers "use glue as a substitute for booze".

WHAT DO INHALANTS DO?

" I saw space invaders which weren't human . . . "

Inhalant users do not really "sniff" the vapours, just into their noses. They inhale, like cigarette smokers inhale, breathing the vapours deep into their lungs. From there the chemicals pass through the thin, moist lining of the lungs into the bloodstream. The blood carries them to the brain and other parts of the body.

Most inhalants are used because they affect the way the brain works. They tend to damp down the part of the brain that controls behaviour. The result is that behaviour becomes less controlled, less "thought about". Under the influence of an inhalant, a person's actions become more spontaneous and immediate.

One major problem is that, although the inhalant may be controllable in quality and quantity, its effects are often unpredictable. They depend on how the person felt beforehand, who he is with, the mood of the group, whether he has eaten a meal recently, and so on. The effects of another powerful drug, alcohol, vary like this too.

Effects on the body – and mind

Most substances that can be inhaled have several effects. The body's breathing and heartbeat slow down. First-timers are often sick and may have headaches.

The main feelings in the mind are of being dazed, drunk or dizzy, floating about and losing touch with reality. Further inhalation produces a feeling of not knowing where you are, sleepiness, numbness, slurred speech and clumsy movements. You lose your balance and find it difficult to walk straight or even sit up properly.

> **The whole world went round, and things went fuzzy and furry. It was so weird ... like being behind frosted glass, nothing in focus.** "

Inhale even more and you may "crash out" or become unconscious. In fact, highly purified forms of some inhaled substances are found in hosptials, where they are used as anaesthetics, to put patients to sleep before an operation.

Funny feelings

Inhalants let behaviour go off the road. Some people

Effects on the brain from solvent abuse.

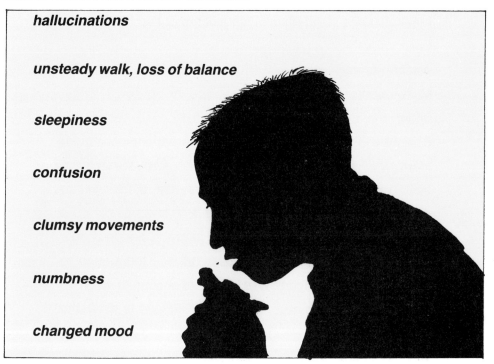

hallucinations

unsteady walk, loss of balance

sleepiness

confusion

clumsy movements

numbness

changed mood

become aggressive, worried that they have lost control. They may get into fights or destroy property.

Others become more friendly. Boys, especially, are often taught not to be too friendly in public. When they inhale, their friendly side comes to the surface (as it may in certain people under the influence of alcohol). People who are usually tough and serious may start finding things funny. They laugh and make jokes when normally they would try to be macho and hard.

Recovery from the state caused by inhaling is normally rapid, within an hour, but there can be problems. Someone on his own may put his head in a bag or under blankets, to increase the effects of the vapours. But he may forget to breathe fresh air, and the air in the bag or under the blankets turns stale, resulting in a coma or even death.

Accidents and inhalants

Most deaths linked to inhalants are accidental. People under the influence seem not to care, and cannot be bothered to take any notice of what is happening around them. This is why sniffing in places such as by rivers, near busy roads, on rooftops or in high-rise blocks is so dangerous.

One boy died when sniffing with a group of friends on a canal bank. He fell into the water and was too stoned to swim. None of his friends was in control enough to stop him from drowning. In another case a boy plunged to his death

Derelict buildings and squats may be used for sniffing sessions.

after he crawled out onto a ledge, high up in a block of flats. He lost his grip and fell.

The effects of mood and hallucinations

As with other drugs, the effects of being stoned on glue or other inhalants vary greatly, depending on the mood at the time. Almost anything is possible, from extreme happiness to starting a fight, sadness, depression, giggles, or increased sexual desire.

Initial happiness may change into a state of confusion and dizziness, ringing in the ears, and changes in sensation including hallucinations (seeing or hearing things which aren't really there). Users have reported seeing shooting stars, witches and devils.

💬💬 *I saw space invaders which weren't human . . . I felt frightened because they were coming at me and I couldn't move.* 💬💬

A girl described one of her friends who had sniffed glue as seeing monkeys all over the floor. The friend tried to climb an imaginary tree to escape. The visions were so real that he kept trying to pick up the monkeys.

Seeing things tends to make the feeling of belonging to a group stronger. Even bad nightmare-like visions may not put off some people, provided they can tell others and have their support. It's like watching a horror film, when you are less scared if you are in a group. Even if you are very frightened you may still want to see more.

Signs on the stairs – a sniffer's used glue tube and plastic bag.

Inhalant users may not be able to control what they do or make judgements properly. As a result they may take part in dangerous "dares" that they wouldn't normally attempt.

More for less

These various effects of inhalants are not the same each time. Unpredictability is a big problem. So is tolerance. This is where the body gradually becomes used to the drug, so that its effects become less and less after repeated use. In order to get back the same feelings of being high, the regular user may need to take higher and higher doses. This increases all the risks.

The methods used

Solvents and other vapours are inhaled in various ways. The simplest method for liquids is direct sniffing from the open end of a bottle. To increase the concentration of the vapours and get a greater effect, some users soak a piece of cloth or cotton wool, or a part of clothing, with the liquid and then put this over the mouth and nose while they breathe in the vapour.

A common way of sniffing glue is to put a little blob of glue in the bottom of an empty plastic bag (often a crisp bag) and then place the open end of the bag over the face, to form a kind of mask. This keeps the vapours concentrated in the bag. But it is dangerous. Apart from the glue vapour itself there is the risk of getting glue on the face or in the eyes, or even of getting glue stuck inside the nose or the mouth.

❝ Sure, glue's dodgy. A guy fell over once and cracked his head, blood everywhere. But what isn't? Crossing the road's dangerous, too. ❞

There are more sophisticated methods that increase the effects of inhalants, which are even more dangerous. They include putting the whole head in a large plastic bag. This is asking for trouble, for if the user passes out and is on his own, he's likely to die from suffocation.

A few people mix inhalants with other drugs such as

Accidental injury is a great risk while under the influence of solvents.

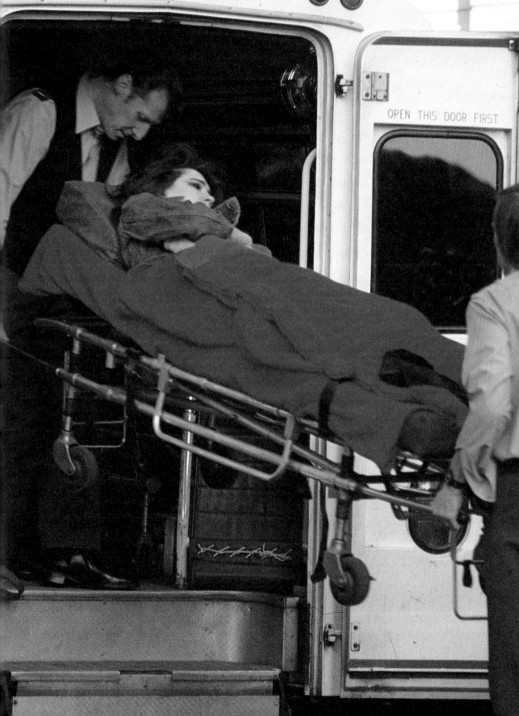

alcohol. The effects are often far more than they bargained for, and the first time may be the last.

Aerosol abuse

Inhaling the solvents and "propellants" in aerosols (the gas which pushes out the paint, or lacquer, or whatever) has become more common recently. Sometimes the spray is aimed up the nose or into the mouth. But the freezing cold gas from an aerosol can cause the throat muscles to seize up, and then there may be swelling and suffocation.

Spraying aerosols onto cloth and then inhaling prevents the breathing in of the paint or deodorant which is carried by the aerosol solvent. Other methods include direct sniffing of cylinders containing cigarette lighter gas or camping gas. This involves the great risk of fire or explosion.

What to do

If you come across someone who may have been sniffing, who is confused or unsteady, take him or her gently to a safe place. Give reassurance. The effects of sniffing usually soon wear off.

ILLNESSES INHALANTS BRING

"They'd sniff it without even looking at the label."

Doctors are well aware of the deadly risks of using inhalants. They have a name for the fatal effects that inhalation has on some people: SSD or "sudden sniffing death". In an SSD the effects of the inhalant, combined with the sudden exertion which it may bring on (such as running or shouting), put great demands on the heart. The heart cannot cope, and it fails.

Sometimes a person may pass out when using inhalants and then be sick, and choke on the vomit. Or, over many years, organs such as the liver and kidneys may be damaged.

❝❝ Why did he do it? We were always telling him about the dangers of plastic bags, from when he was a toddler. Then he used a plastic bag in one of the most dangerous situations of all, sniffing glue. ❞❞

When London doctors looked at nearly 300 inhalant-linked deaths in the UK, they found that over half were caused by the direct poisonous effects of the substance. A quarter of the deaths were due to the throat or lungs being blocked. Glues, aerosols and gas fuels were the main inhalants involved. The risk of death seemed to increase if the sniffer was alone at home.

There are many other risks involved in using inhalants, apart from the ultimate one of dying. They range from temporary effects on health to possible long-term brain damage.

Short-term problems

Users of glue risk an ugly reddening of the skin around the mouth. This is the "sniffer's rash" and is usually caused by the person putting a plastic bag to the nose and mouth, time and time again. The rash consists of red skin, spots and sores, like acne. It usually clears up when the sniffing stops.

People who use inhalants may have runny noses and red, streaming eyes. These are caused by the substance irritating the sensitive lining in the nose and the eye's surface. Such problems usually clear up after a few hours.

Using inhalants regularly can lead to loss of appetite. The person doesn't want to eat very much, so he may

Headlines inform us of the dangers, but do they encourage "copy-cats"?

Plea by parents after girl dies sniffing aerosol

OIL FUMES KILL SNIFFER PALS IN SECRET DEN

BEWARE KILLER SPRAYS

Glue sniff soldier collapses and dies

CANS OF DEATH

SNIFF OF DEATH

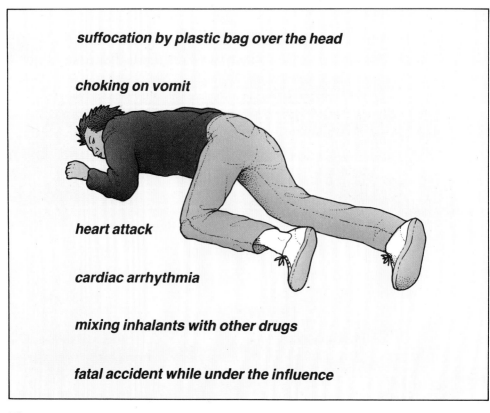

suffocation by plastic bag over the head

choking on vomit

heart attack

cardiac arrhythmia

mixing inhalants with other drugs

fatal accident while under the influence

There are several possible causes of death associated with solvent abuse.

become thin and malnourished. He may also lose interest in his appearance and begin to look dirty and untidy.

Inhalers may also find it hard to sleep well at night, and so they may oversleep in the morning. This can make it difficult for them to hold down a job or get to school on time. They may hang about the house or some other place, looking vacant and listless, and "not caring" what goes on around them. However such behaviour may be due to the problems that led them to sniffing, rather than a result of the sniffing itself.

Sudden effects on the heart

A study of 110 inhalant-linked deaths in the USA found that the most common substances involved were propellants from aerosols. The likeliest explanation for many of the deaths was a condition known as "cardiac arrhythmia". In this, the heart loses its steady, powerful pumping action and begins to beat wildly, with no regular rhythm or pumping effect.

It is thought that the propellant gases in aerosols may multiply the effect of adrenaline (epinephrine), a natural body chemical. Adrenaline helps to cause the so-called "fight or flight" response, which gets the body ready for action when danger threatens. It's when your heart pounds, your face goes pale, your breathing speeds up and your stomach feels "butterflies" when you are frightened.

In a sudden sniffing death the combination of adrenaline and the aerosol gas, coupled with sudden activity, overloads the heart and it fails under the strain.

Suffocation

A person who is suffocating is a terrible sight. He may fall down and writhe about on the ground, slowly turning blue and eventually becoming unconscious. He may choke to death on his own sick if it is not cleared out of his throat. When this happens in a sniffing group, the others are often so horrified and frightened, or so stoned themselves, that they can't do anything to help.

It's difficult to say exactly which inhalants are most likely to cause death by suffocation. The kind of people who die in this way are often heavily involved in inhalants. They may inhale a mixture of vapours, sometimes together with alcohol or another drug.

Glue is still thought to be the most widely used inhalant. (In fact many inhalers do not try anything else.) Glue seems to account for between one quarter and one third of all inhalant-linked deaths. These often involve older users, who are more likely to be heavy users.

But some doctors say that these statistics mean other inhalants, like aerosols and butane gas, are even more dangerous. This is because far fewer people use them, but they cause so many deaths.

Long-term problems and brain damage

The long-term effects of using inhalants are difficult to determine. A Scottish study on over 800 inhalant users found little evidence of long-term damage. In a few cases there were problems, but these cleared up when the sniffing stopped.

It is thought that heavy sniffing of solvents over a long period (perhaps 10 years or more) could damage parts of the brain, especially the regions concerned with the control of movement. This might result in problems such as trembling or shaking and poor balance.

benzene can cause anaemia and leukaemia

dry-cleaning fluid may damage the liver and kidneys

toluene may damage the brain

leaded petrol can result in lead poisoning

butane affects the heart

Different solvents and substances affect different parts of the body.

Sniffing cleaning fluids or aerosols over many years could possibly damage certain other parts of the body, such as the liver or the kidneys.

Many surveys of inhalant abusers have failed to show clear long-term or lasting medical damage. However, surveys of factory workers involved in solvent-based processes have shown some lasting damage to the body. These workers were exposed to high levels every day for many years.

One expert found that solvent inhalers who had been sniffing for ten years or more had the shakes, spoke slowly,

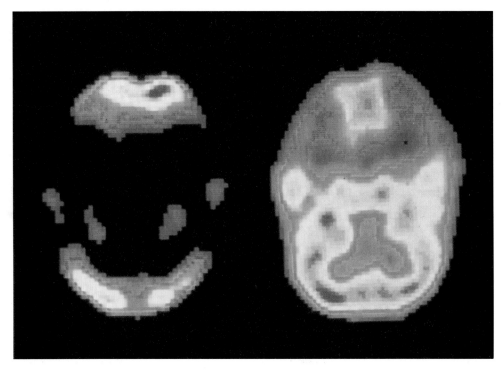

A brain scan shows how heavy drug abuse (left) reduces normal activity.

forgot things, couldn't think straight, and were partially paralysed. Tests on the brains of these people found that in some cases the cortex, the part of the brain linked to our emotions, had shrunk. The part of the brain which controls balance and movement, the cerebellum, had also shrunk in a few of these people.

Inhalants as poisons

Any inhalant can be poisonous, but some of the more unusual solvents are particularly well known for their poisonous effects. Some of them are banned even from chemical laboratories and factories, unless under strict

The typical red eyes and "sniffer's rash" around the mouth.

safety controls. Yet some inhalant users will try them, ignoring all the warnings.

> **Paint, varnish, we'd do the lot. I've heard of kids who'd break into chemists' shops and grab what they can off the shelf. They'd sniff it without even looking at the label.**

The solvent benzene is now known to be poisonous. It used to be common in laboratories, but now it is strictly controlled. It can cause low levels of iron in the blood (anaemia) and leukaemia, a form of blood cancer.

People who inhale petrol fumes risk brain damage from the lead that many countries use as an additive, to improve the performance of car engines. Dry-cleaning and typewriter correction fluids cause damage to the liver and kidneys. Butane (the gas of lighter fuels and camping stoves) is dangerous to the heart. The list of health risks from inhalants, like the list of inhalants themselves, goes on and on.

There are also dangers from the new glues, sprays and other substances coming onto the market. Numerous useful inventions are made in the chemist's laboratory. Of course, new chemicals are exhaustively tested before they can be sold to or used by the public. Yet any damage to the body caused by inhaling may not show up for many years. By that time, the damage might be permanent.

THE COSTS
OF
DEPENDENCE

"Then it seemed like . . . like life and death."

The cost, in money terms, of taking inhalants is not enormous. Some exceptionally heavy users may be getting through 25 or so tubes of glue a day. Even this, compared to drugs like heroin and cocaine, is not much in terms of hard cash.

But it can be enough. People who use inhalants may be still at school, or unemployed. They may have hardly any money of their own. Needing inhalants regularly can lead to all sorts of problems, with family, friends and health, as well as with money.

Do inhalant users become addicts?

It is not clear whether people come to depend physically on inhalants, as they may do with drugs like heroin.

A friendly warning may help to prevent harm later on.

Some British and US experts say that heavy users trying to give up inhalants may have a form of "delirium tremens" or DTs. This is a withdrawal reaction, the sort that alcoholics have when they stop drinking. There is shaking, trembling and sweating, and yearning for the drug. There may be hallucinations, such as seeing bugs or the famous "pink elephants".

What's happened is that the body has become physically used to the drug and needs it to work normally. When the drug is taken away the body is left out of balance and reacts badly.

These experts also said that people could be very irritable and have headaches when they first stopped using in-

halants, after a period of heavy use.

Other experts say the reaction to coming off inhalants is more like a smoker who stops smoking cigarettes. The person may be irritable and tense at first. But after a few days the regular glue sessions aren't missed. The appetite improves and the general appearance shows little trace of former inhalant use. Occasional users, however, should have no reaction when they give up.

However, research shows that some inhalant users may need higher and higher doses of the inhalant to get high. This can happen after getting dosed up just once a

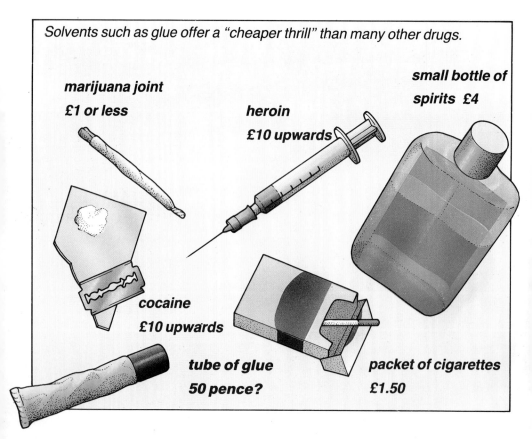

Solvents such as glue offer a "cheaper thrill" than many other drugs.

marijuana joint
£1 or less

heroin
£10 upwards

small bottle of
spirits £4

cocaine
£10 upwards

tube of glue
50 pence?

packet of cigarettes
£1.50

week for as little as three months. Needing bigger doses for the same effect is called tolerance. Bigger doses multiply all the risks connected with inhalant use.

Psychological dependence

So much for the body. What about the mind? Research also shows that some users find it difficult to give up inhalants. They need help and advice in order to kick the habit. This shows there is some "psychological" dependence. These people need inhalants to get them through the day. Their minds come to depend on the feelings they get from inhalants. This sort of dependence can be just as real as the physical dependence of the body.

Stealing to keep the habit

Some people turn to crime to pay for their inhaling. This might be stealing money from others in their family to buy supplies, or stealing glue or other inhalants directly from shops. Some break into factories to get at solvents or other inhalants used in industry. They siphon off a small amount from a large storage drum, hoping that the missing amount won't be noticed.

❝ Bill worked for a few months in a chemical factory. He did nights. I reckon he kept half the town sniffing. ❞

In one survey, involving more than a hundred heavy users, 12 said they had stolen things from home and sold

No school today? The face of guilt . . . truanting to sniff with friends.

them to buy inhalants. They had also stolen goods from shops. However the amounts of money involved are usually small, so these cases don't usually attract much attention. All the headlines go on heroin busts or cocaine smuggling.

The costs to the individual

The real costs of dependence lie in the effects of inhalants on the user's life. Heavy users often argue with their parents about their sniffing and its effects in causing violent and aggressive behaviour. This may just make things worse, because the user may then inhale even more to try and get away from the trouble at home.

But getting high is no answer. It blocks the kind of straight thinking which helps sort out problems. The cost of continuing to use inhalants can be a miserable life centred on blotting out everything.

A few users go to great lengths to maintain a source of supply for their habit. One broke out of his house in the middle of the night and woke up a friend, asking for glue. Another also ran to a friend's house for more glue – without any clothes on. His parents had taken away his clothes to try and stop him sniffing.

❝ *I had to do it. I just had to. I needed it, I needed to get high. Now, I can't see why. Then, it seemed like . . . like life and death.* ❞

Tell-tale signs of inhalant abuse

If you suspect someone of sniffing solvents, aerosols, glue or similar substances, there are several tell-tale signs which include:

- *changed behaviour, such as being giggly, silly, rowdy, or "drunk" as though on alcohol*
- *red or runny eyes, runny nose*
- *spots and sores around the mouth*
- *smell of chemicals on the breath and clothes*
- *stains or marks on the clothes*
- *reacting violently when questioned, showing guilt feelings*
- *telling lies about being with friends, skipping school or*

work, not turning up for appointments
- drowsiness, generally confused, trouble getting to sleep, sleeping late and having problems getting up
- possessing glue tubes, aerosols, solvent bottles, plastic bags and similar items
- stealing, asking for or borrowing money, always broke

Who are the "sniffers"?

The statistics show that in the UK most inhalant users are boys, and most are between 12 and 16 years of age. Some teenagers see glue as "their" drug, whereas adults have alcohol and tobacco. After the age of 25 to 30 years very few people continue.

❝❝ It came to our school once. A few people did it, for a few weeks. But a couple of them got caught and it all died out. ❞❞

CAN INHALANT ABUSE BE STOPPED?

"... restricting sales cannot be the whole answer."

Could inhalant abuse ever be stopped? Banning the sale of all substances which can be inhaled would be almost impossible. It would remove from the shops too many useful household products. It is estimated that "sniffable" substances are sold in around 190,000 shops in the UK.

A selective ban

Buying tobacco is illegal if you are under a certain age. Would this sort of law work with glue and other inhaled substances? Banning the sale of glue to young people, say those under 16, would be unfair to those using products for their intended purpose. What about the children who like making models or enjoy craft hobbies?

A ban like this may encourage inhalant users to turn to other, possibly more dangerous, substances. The average home contains around 30 different solvent-based substances which could be sniffed. It would be difficult to stop a determined user from getting his hands on something to inhale.

Restricting sales

Some countries place an obligation on shopkeepers. They should not supply inhalants to young people if they think they are going to sniff them.

A form of this law exists in England. Under the Intoxicating Substances (Supply) Act of 1985, shopkeepers and others are not permitted to supply people under 18 years of age with substances which could be inhaled, if the supplier knows or has reasonable cause to believe that the substance is likely to be used for the purpose of intoxication (getting drunk or high).

Shopkeepers in England have been found guilty and fined for selling butane gas to young boys.

Two Scottish shopkeepers were found guilty under a separate law, of supplying "glue kits" to young people. They broke the law openly, despite warnings from the police. They sold blobs of glue, from a stock of several gallons, in crisp bags. Few shopkeepers break the law like this so the number of prosecutions has been small.

But restricting sales cannot be the whole answer. Inhalant users can get their supplies from other places. Some steal solvents from factories, hospitals, schools and shops. This was seen in Glasgow, in Scotland. When shopkeepers there set up their own voluntary ban on selling inhalable substances to under-age children, there was a rash of break-ins and burglaries.

Suspicious signs

Shopkeepers who sell aerosols, glue and other inhalant-type substances have responded to public concern. In many countries their trade associations have produced guidelines to help reduce inhalant abuse. The guidelines warn staff in shops and stores to look out for groups of young people standing around counters where inhalants are sold, and to watch for individuals who keep buying inhalants.

Many shops, especially DIY stores, carry warning notices saying that they reserve the right not to sell certain solvent-based goods. Hopefully the warnings put off abusers and make it more difficult for them to get their supplies.

If there is an inhalant "craze" in an area, some shops will keep sniffable products under strict control. They put them on high shelves, or behind the counter or in a back room, so that the buyer must ask for them.

A horrible-smelling additive?
Some people give up smoking by taking tablets which make cigarettes taste revolting. The same principle could be used with inhalants. Some form of horrible-smelling additive could be put into inhalant products to make them too unpleasant to breathe in.

But this proposal, designed to curb inhalant abuse, would also put off the ordinary consumer. And every single product capable of being sniffed would have to contain the smelly additive. Finding something which worked well on a range of products, and which itself was not flammable, and did not cause allergies or pose a risk to health from ordinary use, would be a difficult task – maybe even impossible. Scientists at the UK's Ministry of Defence tried to find such an "aversive" substance but found nothing really suitable.

What about warning labels?
Another option is to put warning labels or stickers on all sniffable items. But this only draws attention to them, and to sniffing in general. It would also tell inhalant users which new substances they could abuse.

Warning notices hopefully make inhalant users think again.

UHU All Purpose
Strong clear adhesive

UHU All P
Strong cle

UHU All F
Strong Gl

UHU All Purpose
Stron clear

87p

UHU All Pu

GLUE WILL
NOT BE SOLD
TO CHILDREN

PLAY
SAFE
"TH

"childsplay"
ADHESIVE

WA
OI

Outlawing the "high"

In many countries it is not actually against the law to be high on solvents, in private or in public. Should the law be changed?

Many people say no. Outlawing inhalant "drunkenness" could make criminals of thousands of young people. Being arrested and punished by fines or prison may not be the best answer – providing, of course, other laws on theft, assault and so on are not broken. Advice and help from a combination of social workers, educational experts and medical staff is often a better way to deal with inhalant abuse.

Manufacturers join the battle

The manufacture of substances that can be abused as inhalants is a perfectly legal activity. But the abuse has worried industry. Makers of glue and other solvent-based products have come up with ways to reduce the possibility of abuse.

One UK manufacturer of polystyrene cement, the sort of glue used to make model aeroplanes, has added a new substance to the glue's formula, which causes soreness and irritation if it is breathed too much. The manufacturer says that customers wanting to use the glue for its proper purpose have readily accepted the new formula. Only continuous sniffers are irritated by the additive.

Another approach, especially for glues, is to remove the most harmful solvents and use water-based glues instead. You can't get high on water. But while the formula of some glues can be changed in this way, other types of glue do not work without solvents.

The lessons of history

Sniffing substances like ether and chloroform has a long history going back to the 1800s. But the modern sniffing craze started in the USA in the 1950s, after a Denver newspaper ran a series of sensational stories about glue sniffing. (This pattern has been repeated several times: when inhalants hit the headlines, there is a local outbreak of

Banning glues would hit many enjoyable pastimes such as plane-making.

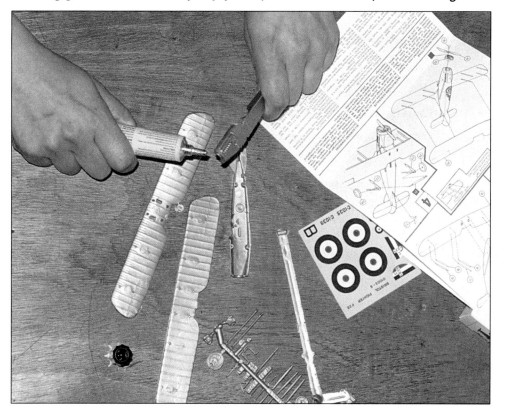

sniffing soon after.)

The problem got worse, and in New York in the 1960s new laws were brought in. They banned the sale of solvent-based glues to anyone under the age of 18 unless they were sold as part of a model-making kit. Selling glue to anyone for the purpose of intoxication was also made a criminal offence.

Some US states followed New York with even tougher laws, making it an offence to sniff certain inhalants, mainly glues. The punishment could be 11 months in jail. But the ban had some tragic results as people switched to other, more dangerous inhalants such as aerosols, and died.

Other laws required manufacturers to list those substances which could be misused by inhalation. This was a great help to the sniffers!

In general, there were two types of law. One banned the selling, the other the smelling, of inhalants. In the end, neither type of law had much effect. Legislation against glue sniffing only seemed to encourage experiments with other, more dangerous inhalants. And laws banning sniffing itself were difficult to enforce in practice. Like the prohibition laws brought in against alcohol many years before, they did not really work.

The main problem facing those who make such laws is that trying to control what the ordinary citizen does is difficult. In democratic countries people do not like having their lives restricted. Attempts to stop inhalant abuse have often made things worse by driving it underground.

GETTING HELP

❝ It is important to make inhalant users aware of the risks. ❞

Asking for help is nothing to be ashamed of. We all need help in some way, every day.

So what if you've been doing a bit of glue, and now that you've read this far, you want to stop? You could finish hanging around with the glue crowd and find some new friends, or just say you don't want to sniff any more. If you do that, you'll be like plenty of other people who have used inhalants for a short time and then stopped. Inhalants do not seem to be physically addictive, so you should not be ill if you stop.

Someone to help

Many inhalant users feel they can't stop on their own. Perhaps most of their friends sniff, and they don't want to lose all their friends. If this is the case, the best thing to do is to approach someone you trust. Parent, aunt or uncle, teacher, leader at the local youth group, family doctor, priest – anyone you feel easy with. If you think hard enough there's probably someone who will be ready to listen and help. If you show them you really do want to stop, people will be more understanding than you think.

❛❛ If only he'd come to us . . . we had no idea he was taking solvents, we'd have helped. Maybe he was too scared of us. ❜❜

Using inhalants in itself is not a crime. Surprisingly for many users, the police are usually helpful and knowledgable. They want to advise users before their problems become to great, because overall it saves them work in the long run.

If you can't think of anyone at all, every area has people who know how to help you. Their names, addresses and telephone numbers are given near the end of the book.

Helping a friend

Maybe you want help not for yourself, but for a friend who is abusing inhalants. If you do know someone like this, don't panic. The chances are that it's not going to kill them, especially if they do it only occasionally. The main danger is an accident.

But it is important to make inhalant users aware of the risks. The best help you can give is to tell them the sort of information contained in this book.

Finding out why

People usually sniff glue in groups, so if your friend is sniffing alone, it is a bit more worrying. Try and find out if something in particular is worrying him, or if he is depressed or in trouble.

The solvent abuse organizations are experts at getting to the root of the problem. Sniffing may be a symptom of some underlying problem. When this is sorted out, there no longer seems any need for inhalants.

Friends may be able to help in sorting things out. We all have problems from time to time. Trying to ecape them or block them out by inhaling is not an answer.

"Solvents . . . are not the solution."

FACTFILE

Abusing volatile substances such as chloroform and ether has a long history, going back to the 1800s. The modern sniffing craze began in the 1950s, when a newspaper in Denver, USA, ran a series of sensational articles about sniffing glue. Since then the practice of solvent abuse has hit the headlines every few years or so. However, there seems to be a steady level of "background" solvent abuse in most countries.

Tube and bag, signs of abuse.

The science of solvents

Many substances which can be abused by inhaling are known scientifically as solvents. Inhalant abuse is often called solvent abuse.

Solvents are substances that dissolve others. The solvents that are abused are the ones which evaporate (turn from a liquid into a vapour or gas) easily, often at normal temperatures. Such solvents are useful as "carriers" of, for example, a paint. When the paint-and-solvent combination is applied to a surface the solvent slowly evaporates, leaving behind the paint itself – a process we refer to as paint drying.

This volatile nature of certain substances makes them useful but also abusable by inhaling.

What to do

If you come across someone who has passed out due to inhaling, keep calm. Make sure he can breathe fresh air by removing any bag near the mouth and nose or opening the windows. If he does not recover consciousness in a few minutes, get emergency medical help. Provided he is not injured, place him in the recovery position shown below. This way, if he is sick there is less chance of him choking on the vomit.

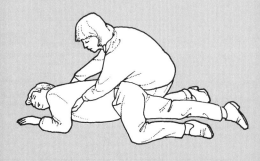

DRUG PROFILE

Substances inhaled	Glues and adhesives, paints, lacquers, thinners, typing correction fluid, paint stripper, dry-cleaning fluid, anti-freeze, nail varnish remover, gas lighter refills, camping gas, dyes, polishes, aerosols of various kinds (hair spray and lacquer, air freshener, fly spray, deodorant, anti- perspirant), and many others
Where they occur	In the average household are some 30 substances that can be abused by inhaling; some shops and stores, especially DIY centres, sell dozens of them
Ways of taking	Direct sniffing from the end of the container; vapours may be concentrated in a plastic bag, under a blanket; substance may be put on material which is held up to the nose and mouth
Speed of action	Act very quickly, often within a few seconds, bringing the risk of an accident
Common effects	A type of drunkenness, silly or giggly behaviour, slurred speech, unsteady movements, red eyes, runny nose, aggression, violence, passing out
Dangers	Accidents from losing control in an unsafe place, suffocation, choking on vomit, various health risks to the heart, kidneys and other vital organs, possibility of brain damage
Dependence	Not clear if physical dependence occurs; a few users become psychologically dependent
Legal status	Inhalant abuse itself is not illegal in many countries, although the behaviour and events it may lead to could be unlawful (vandalism, disorderly or threatening behaviour, fighting); in some countries, selling glues and other substances to under-age people is not allowed if the supplier suspects they will be abused

SOURCES OF HELP

Here are addresses and telephone numbers of organizations that might be able to help people with an inhalant problem.

Specialists in inhalant abuse

Kick-It (National Office)
6 Church Street, Wolverton, Milton Keynes MK2 5JN
Telephone Milton Keynes (0908) 368869 or 0924 477146
National Campaign Against Solvent Abuse
245A Coldharbour Lane, London SW9
Telephone London (01) 274 7700 ext 22
Re-Solv, The Society for the Prevention of Solvent and Volatile Substance Abuse
St Mary's Chambers, 19 Station Road, Stone, Staffs ST15 8JP
Telephone Stone (0785) 817885 or 46097
National Association of Young Peoples' Counselling and Advisory Services
17-23 Albany Street, Leicester LE1 6CD
Telephone Leicester (0533) 554775
National Children's Bureau
8 Wakley Street, London EC1V 7QE
Telephone London (01) 278 9441-7

Regional centres

Many of the above organizations, such as Re-Solv and the National Campaign Against Solvent Abuse, will put you in touch with local advisers who can help. Local branches of the Citizens' Advice Bureau and the Samaritans (look for their numbers in the local phone book) can also put you in touch with advisers.

Drug helplines

From anywhere in Britain, dial 100 and ask for Freephone Drug Problems. Calls are free and confidential, and you will get advice on where to go for help.

Up-to-date information

An important source of information on where to get help is:

The Standing Conference on Drug Abuse (SCODA)
1-4 Hatton Place, London EC1N 8ND
Telephone London (01) 430 2341
SCODA can provide a list of local drug advice centres.

General health information

Health Education Authority
78 New Oxford Street,
London WC1A 1AH
Telephone London (01) 631 0930
The authority provides a selection of pamphlets, booklets and leaflets, on the risks of drug abuse as well as on other health matters. In Scotland:
Scottish Health Education Group
Health Education Centre,
Woodburn House, Canaan Lane,
Edinburgh EH10 4SG
Telephone Edinburgh (031) 447 8044

Information on inhalants

Institute for the Study of Drug Dependence (ISDD)
address as for SCODA (above)
Telephone London (01) 430 1991
ISDD provides information on the risks of using solvents and other inhalants.

In Australia

Each state and some major cities have an Alcohol and Drug Information Service. Phone them for details:

Sydney	*(02) 3312111*
NSW Country	*(008) 422599*
Aus Cap Ter	*(062) 491421*
South Aus	*(08) 2743391*
Melbourne	*(03) 6141999*
Victoria Country	*(008) 136385*
Brisbane	*(07) 2292877*
Qld Country	*(008) 177833*
Western Aus	*(09) 4811088*
Northern Ter	*(089) 818030*
Tasmania	*(002) 345600*

WHAT THE WORDS MEAN

acetone solvent commonly found in glues and nail varnish removers

addict someone who needs to keep taking a drug in order to remain "normal" and stave off withdrawal effects on the body and/or mind. "Addiction" has a slightly different meaning to "dependence", in that it usually refers to someone who has been dependent on a drug for some time, and it is more tied up with his lifestyle and society's view of him. In some countries "addict" is a legal term, meaning someone who's registered on an official list as being dependent on a drug. This term is not generally used when talking about inhalants

aerosol can containing a product (perfume, deodorant, paint, hair spray, etc.), a solvent and a propellant which pushes the product out of the can as a fine spray

benzene solvent used in some glues and in petrol, in some countries

butane gas found in camping-gas bottles and gas-lighter refills

cardiac arrhythmia wild out-of-time and uncoordinated heartbeats. Can be caused by sniffing and may result in death

dependence the need to keep taking a drug regularly, either for its effects on the body (to keep away withdrawal symptoms, for instance) or its effects on the mind (such as to make the user think he is "getting through the day"). Any dependence caused by inhalants is largely psychological

drug any chemical or other substance that changes the body's workings (including the way the person's mind works, his behaviour, etc.)

drug abuse non-medical drug use with harmful effects, on the abuser and possibly on others

drug misuse using drugs in a way which people in general would see as not sensible, or not acceptable, and possibly harmful

inhalant gas, fumes or vapour that can be breathed into the lungs and that has intoxicating effects on the brain

intoxication state of being "drunk" or "high" on a drug, not in full control

sniffing when applied to inhalants, breathing the vapours in through the nose and down into the lungs

solvent substance that dissolves and "carries" another (glue, for example) and then evaporates (as the glue dries). Many solvents give off vapours which can be inhaled

SSD Sudden Sniffing Death, which is death by heart failure immediately after a sniffing session

tolerance when the body becomes used to a drug, so that the same dose begins to have less effect, and increasing doses must be taken for the same effect

toluene solvent commonly found in glue

vapour gas or fumes, given off by a solvent, for example

volatile liquid or solid which evaporates easily giving off vapour

withdrawal the effects on the body and mind when a person suddenly stops taking a drug after being dependent on it. The effects are usually unpleasant

INDEX

accident 22, 59
acetone 61
addict 40, 61
adrenaline 33
aerosol 28, 34, 61
alcohol 12, 20, 28
amphetamines 5
anaemia 37
anaesthetic 21
Australia 60

benzene 37, 61
body 20
boredom 14
brain 12, 30, 38
butane 34, 38, 61

cardiac arrhythmia 33, 61
Citizens' Advice Bureau 60
cocaine 40
coma 22
crime 43

death 22, 30, 33
delirium tremens 40
Denver 53
dependence 43, 59, 61
drug 5, 12, 61

epinephrine 33

Freephone Drug Problems 60

Glasgow 49
glue 34
glue sniffing 8, 26

hallucination 24, 40
Health Education Authority 60
heart 33
help 56, 59
heroin 5, 10, 40
high 8, 12, 52

inhalant 5, 59, 61
  cost 40
  effects 12, 20, 30, 59
  manufacture 52
  signs of abuse 45
  type of user 16
inhaling 20
  methods of 26
Intoxicating Substances Act 48
ISDD 60

Kick-It 60

legal status 59
legislation 54

marijuana 11
mind 20, 43
Ministry of Defence 51

National Association of Young People's Counselling and Advisory Services 60
National Campaign Against Solvent Abuse 60

National Children's Bureau 60
New York 54

poison 30, 36

recovery 22
Re-Solv 60

Samaritans 60
SCODA 60
Scotland 49
Scottish Health Education Authority 60
sniffer's rash 31
sniffing 26, 61
solvent 5, 61
stoned 8, 12
Sudden Sniffing Death 30, 61
suffocation 26, 33, 59

tobacco 17
tolerance 25, 43, 61
toluene 61

UK 46, 48
USA 53, 54
US Solvent Abuse Helpline 15

vapour 5, 12, 20, 26, 61

withdrawal 40, 61

Photographic Credits:
Cover and pages 14-15 and 47: Network Photographers; pages 4, 16, 23 (inset), 27 and 44: Rex Features; pages 7, 9, 35 and 55: Janine Weidel; page 13: Frank Spooner Agency; page 19, 25, 29, 37, 39, 53 and 58: Vanessa Bailey; pages 23 and 40-41: Robert Harding; page 31: John Frost Newspapers; page 36: Science Photo Library; page 51: John Hillelson Agency.